INTERIOR COLOR BY DESIGN

A design tool for architects, interior designers, and homeowners

GLOUCESTER MASSACHUSETTS

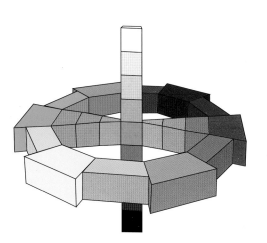

JONATHAN POORE

ROCKPORT PUBLISHERS

IN MEMORY OF RICHARD POORE, JR.

First published in the United States of America by:
Rockport Publishers, Inc.
33 Commercial Street
Gloucester, Massachusetts 01930
Telephone: (978) 282-9590
Fax: (978) 283-2742
www.rockpub.com

First Singapore edition published 1994 by
Rockport Publishers, Inc. for:
The Bookshop Pte, Ltd.
Blk 4, Pasir Panjang Road
08-33 Alexandra Distripark
Singapore 0511
Telephone: (65) 2730128
Fax: (65) 2730042

ISBN 1-56496-037-4

10 9 8 7 6

Printed in China

Illustrations by Jonathan Poore

CONTENTS

INTRODUCTION

he primary goal of *Interior Color By Design* is to equip the professional designer as well as the homeowner with the tools and understanding to use color effectively in architectural and interior design. It is designed to be used as a reference manual, an actual tool, to experiment with and design color schemes. Part I outlines the basics of color theory as they apply to interior design. Each principle of color theory is illustrated with specific examples of richly colored interiors to both explain the theory as well as spark the imagination. Part II, a virtual library of color ideas, is a compilation of sample color combinations. Each type of color scheme is shown in a sample interior and is followed with color chips showing variations on that color theme.

The greatest challenge in color design is to be able to predict and control the result of a color scheme. Effective color selection can be an inexpensive yet powerful element in any design. Color can perform a multitude of roles and can affect a person's emotions, energy level, and sense of order, or disorder. As well, it can set the tone of an interior and make it seem formal or informal, masculine or feminine, cooly aloof or invitingly warm. The aim of successful interior color design is to be able to control these effects through the masterful use of color as a design tool itself. *Interior Color By Design* outlines some basic techniques that take the mystery out of the color design process.

Color design can never be reduced to a science, but by becoming familiar with some basic rules of color theory it is possible to find a comfortable "jumping-off" point. With a basic understanding of color theory it is possible to apply the rules fairly literally and come up with conservative but successful color schemes. As a person's skill and confidence increases, it is possible to take a more intuitive approach to color design, often bending the rules for more imaginative effects.

To communicate in words the subtle differences between individual colors is always difficult; there are virtually an infinite number of color combinations. To understand color and design with color, it is essential to have a basic knowledge of color theory. The first step in an organized understanding of color is to learn about the basic attributes and how they can be used to achieve dramatic and effective color design.

PART I

ATTRIBUTES OF COLOR

HUE OR COLOR

The first attribute of color is *hue*, which is the name for a color, such as yellow, green, blue, red. The color wheel is used to represent the basic colors (hues) of the visible spectrum. All the hues indicated on the color wheel are of full intensity. For the sake of simplicity, the most common color wheel is made up of 12 color gradations, even though there are actually an infinite number of color gradations possible between each color on the wheel.

VALUE OR LIGHTNESS

The second attribute of color is *value*, or the relative lightness or darkness of a color. Lighter values are achieved by adding white to a color, and darker values result from adding black.

CHROMA OR SATURATION

The third attribute of color is *chroma*, or *saturation*, the relative purity or intensity of a color determined by how much or how little gray is added to the color. The *value* of the colors on a chroma scale do not change; only the *intensity* of the color varies.

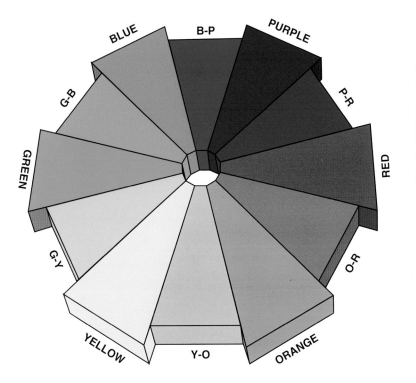

Fig. 1.1 *Color wheel*

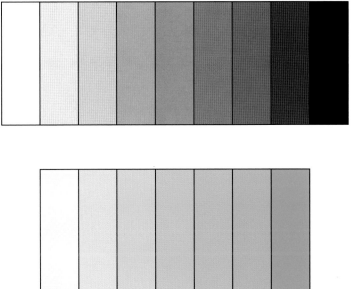

Fig. 1.2 *Gray value scale and green value scale*

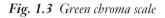

Fig. 1.3 *Green chroma scale*

FULL INTENSITY   **TINT**

So, the three attributes of color— hue, value, and chroma—are what defines every color. Albert Munsell, the color theorist, describes each and every color as having three dimensions; therefore, to fully describe any color it is necessary to describe each of these dimensions or attributes.

SHADE   **TONE**

Fig. 1.5 *Tint, shade, and tone of red*

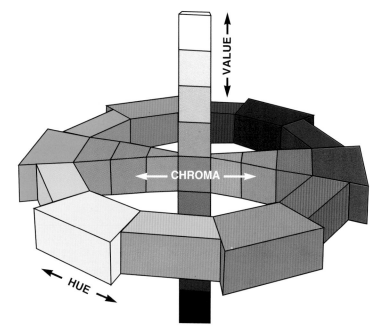

Fig. 1.4 *Hue, value, and chroma—the three dimensions of color*

OTHER COLOR TERMS

Other color terms useful to a basic understanding of color theory are **tint, shade,** *and* **tone**. *All of these are colors of full intensity or chroma mixed with white, black, or some value of gray. Mixing with white creates a tint (pastels), mixing with black produces a shade, and combining some value of gray with another color creates a tone.*

COLOR TEMPERATURE

Colors are often referred to as either warm or cool. The colors on the color wheel are easy to separate into warm and cool colors. Red, orange, and yellow are considered warm while green, blue, and purple are described as cool. As colors become less pure, the terms *warm* and *cool* become more useful as relative comparisons rather than absolute descriptions.

HOW COLORS MIX

ADDITIVE COLOR

Natural light contains all the colors of the spectrum. By breaking light down into its component parts, or spectral colors, it is possible to combine and mix the individual colors to form new ones. *Additive color* is the process of mixing colored light. The most common application of this can be found in theater lighting. For example, a red light overlapping a green light produces a yellow light. Colored pigments, however, behave very differently than colored light when combined or mixed. The primary colors of light are red, green, and blue; the primary colors of pigments are red, yellow, and blue. When all three primary colors of light are combined, they form white light, and, when two colors of light are added together they always produce a color of lighter value.

The principles of additive color are most critical in theater or other dramatic lighting. For the purposes of interior color design, it is important to understand the effect of artificial lighting on the perception of color. For example, incandescent light brings out the warm colors of an interior while fluorescent light emphasizes the cool colors.

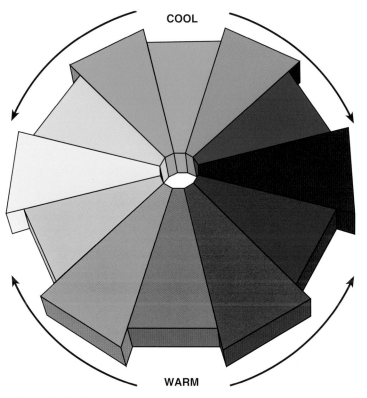

Fig. 1.6 *Cool and warm colors*

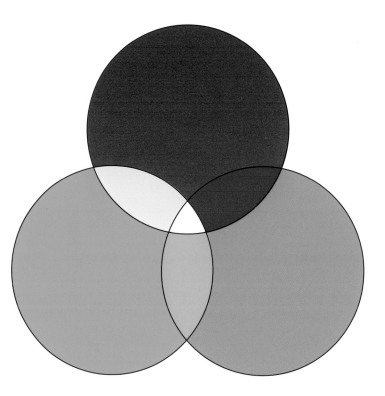

Fig. 1.7 *Additive color*

11

The decorative paper on the ceiling is lit with a relatively cool fluorescent light hidden in the soffit. Note how the cool light reduces the intensity of the warm red flowers yet does not affect the cool green foliage in the pattern. The incandescent dome light on the ceiling casts a warm yellow glow over the white ceiling in sharp contrast to the cool white appearance of the same paint finish illuminated by the fluorescent light.

12

SUBTRACTIVE COLOR

Subtractive color is the result of mixing pigments, dyes, or other colorants. The apparent color of a surface is based on what part of the visible spectrum of light is absorbed versus what portion is reflected back to the viewer. Since the main concern of this book is the color of interior finishes, and not lighting, the focus will be on subtractive, rather than additive, color.

The *primary* subtractive colors are red, yellow, and blue. These are called *primary* colors because all other colors are derived from some combination of these three. When all three primary colors are combined in equal amounts the resulting color is a deep, blackish brown. Note that the primary colors are spaced exactly equidistant from one another on the color wheel. Midway between each primary color is what is called a *secondary* color.

When two adjacent primary colors are mixed together they form the *secondary* color found between them on the color wheel. For example, yellow and blue paint mixed together makes green. The other secondary colors are orange (red and yellow combined) and purple (red and blue combined). When adjacent primary and secondary colors are mixed, they form *tertiary* colors. Between each of the six primary and secondary colors are the *tertiary* colors consisting of red-orange, orange-yellow, yellow-green, green-blue, blue-purple, and purple-red.

PARTITIVE COLOR

When a very consistent, fine pattern of two distinct colors is viewed from a slight distance, the eye tends to mix the colors optically and derive a third color. This is called *partitive* color.

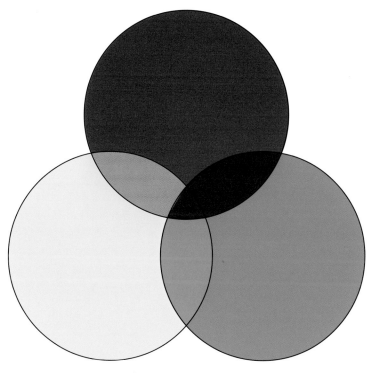

Fig. 1.8 *Subtractive colors*

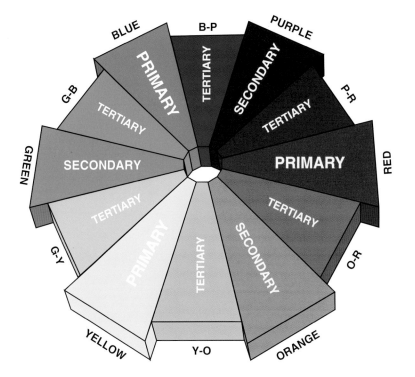

Fig. 1.9 *Color wheel with primaries, secondaries, and tertiaries labeled*

13

A commonly used example of partitive color is the post-Impressionist painting technique of pointillism, where small dots or "points" of different colors are placed on the canvas to create an extremely rich, vibrant color. In architectural color, the greatest richness and depth is achieved with partitive color mixing, such as in glazing or in the stippling techniques of decorative painting. The subtle, multicolor effects of stone or wood are examples of partitive color used in natural materials. When granite is viewed very closely, numerous shades of gray are apparent, yet when viewed from a distance, all the little specks of color blend to form a complex, rich gray which would be unachievable with a uniformly colored surface.

Although the color of the accent walls in each of these photos is very similar, the effect achieved is remarkably different. The red-orange wall in the above photo has a strong graphic quality to it because the color is flat and solid. The walls in the photo on the facing page are glazed to achieve richness and depth. The glazing is a mixture of two distinct colors that the human eye then blends together to form one richly textured color.

CHAPTER 2: ARCHITECTURAL CONSIDERATIONS IN COLOR DESIGN

COLOR AS AN ARCHITECTURAL DESIGN INGREDIENT

Architectural and interior design consists of the manipulation of many interrelated elements including space, form, structure, light, texture, and color. Unfortunately, the one ingredient in the interdependent mix of design elements that is most often overlooked or left as an afterthought is color. To avoid this, approach color selection as an integral part of the design rather than something which is applied superficially after the fact.

Effective color design does not need to add any cost to interior renovations or construction: it is a simple matter of planning ahead. The best approach is to look at all the paint colors and other materials as a single color composition.

The most successful interior color design is responsive and appropriate to the design goals. Some of the important roles color can play include

1. Setting the emotional tone or ambiance of a space

2. Focusing or diverting attention

3. Modulating the space to feel larger or smaller

4. Breaking up and defining the space

5. Unifying the space or knitting it together

Setting the emotional tone. *The colors in the lively living room on the facing page project an energetic sense of whimsy.*

The cool and somewhat somber green, gray, and black lend an air of calm sophistication to this dining room which is then balanced with the warm inviting glow of the colored glass windows.

Focusing or diverting attention. *The red and yellow accent colors of the display cabinet help weave together the collection of objects which also include splashes of red and yellow. The delightful decorative border on the wall mimics the shapes and colors of the display items in miniature.*

Muted colors and rich materials give the otherwise complex space below a sense of order and restfulness.

Modulating the space to feel larger or smaller.
The light colors of this alcove are made more soft and luminous by being indirectly lit from above. This adds a dimension of airy spaciousness to this cozy little seating area. Darker colors without indirect lighting would have made this space feel very closed in.

Below, the dark intensity of the red walls and ceiling give this room a powerful sense of containment and formality.

What would have been an otherwise uncomfortably tall and narrow space is given a pleasant sense of scale by painting the ceiling a deep color and accenting the architectural moldings. The dark green ceiling has the visual effect of reducing the apparent height of the ceiling.

Below, a simple, unadorned room with a high ceiling can be transformed inexpensively by adding a picture molding. This simple addition to the space opens up many possible places for color. The wall above the molding is painted in a muted accent color and a small portion of the molding profile is highlighted with a deep gold accent. Note that the strongest colors are used in the smallest amounts.

Unifying the space or knitting it together. *Color is used here to highlight each architectural element in the space as though it is a freestanding piece of furniture. The overall harmony of the color scheme keeps these individual furniture elements unified. The contrasting accent colors emphasize the different layers of room-dividing elements which create an even greater illusion of depth and space, much like a lively stage set. The figure dancing across the frieze panel adds to this theatrical quality.*

Breaking up and defining the space. *Color in this interior helps organize and accent the exposed roof structure. The cool gray ceiling provides a subtle contrast against the warm brown of the walls and rafter beams.*

21

INTERACTIVENESS OF COLOR RELATIONSHIPS

Colors cannot be selected without taking into account all of the adjacent colors and materials in the space. This requires examining the total environment where the colors will be used. Adjacent colors can have a very strong effect on one another; therefore, it is important to be able to predict and control their interaction. By itself, a very muted color often looks absolutely neutral. Yet when placed against another contrasting, muted color, both appear to come alive and be stronger colors.

Fig. 2.2 *Cool gray*

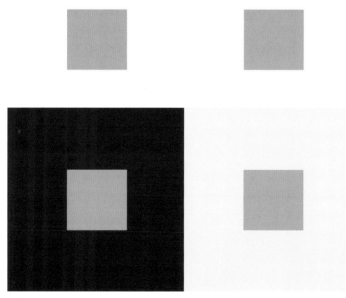

Fig. 2.1 *The same color against two different color backgrounds appears to change hue*

Fig. 2.3 *The same cool gray against a warm white makes the gray appear blue*

The consistent, monochromatic grays of this interior make the colors appear absolutely neutral because there are no warm or cool accent colors for the grays to react with. This gives the space a formal, sculptural yet abstract quality.

The gray walls in this room are similar to the grays in the photo on the right, yet the walls appear more blue than gray because they are contrasted against the creamy white trim.

The soft hint of taupe in the wall would be lost if it were not for the blue accent wall and the pale blue-green cushion adjacent to it. The interactiveness of the adjacent colors is what lends this interior its subtle richness.

Each of the colors in this interior is fairly muted. The colors react together to form a deep, rich golden tone on the walls with a soft blue accent.

The warm wood tones bring out the subtle lavender cast in the off-white walls, giving the space a fresh, airy feeling.

24

COLOR HIERARCHY AND PROPORTIONS

The hues of the color wheel form a hierarchy, with some hues being naturally more dominant than others, even when used in precisely the same proportions. It is fairly easy to see which colors are dominant on the color wheel. As different values and chroma are introduced, the hierarchies become more complex. Changing the individual proportions of the selected colors also affects which color dominates. It is helpful to know which color will dominate in any given combination of colors. Below are a few general principles to help guide the designer.

DOMINANT HUES

When viewed together, warm colors appear to advance while cool colors appear to recede. This is especially true when the different colors are viewed in similar proportions. The warmer colors actually trigger a different *physiological* response in the eye than the cool colors do: this is why the warm colors appear to be in the foreground. Warmer colors also elicit a stronger *psychological* reaction: red, orange, and yellow are naturally more arousing and exciting than the more subdued and soothing blue, green, and purple.

Fig. 2.4 *Primary red, yellow, and blue swatches of equal size show that the red advances and is dominant while the blue and yellow recede and are subordinate.*

When red, yellow, and blue are viewed together in equal proportions the red dominates and appears to advance. The yellow is next in dominance while the blue is least dominant.

DOMINANT CHROMA

Purer colors advance and dominate, while muted or grayed tones of the same color recede. Again, this assumes that the two colors appear in approximately equal proportions. Remember, the eye is naturally drawn to colors which are more intense.

It is helpful to know which color dominates so that it is not used in such a great quantity as to overpower the other colors in the scheme. Understanding which color advances and which recedes can be useful if a greater apparent depth of space is desired. Intense colors can be used in the foreground while more subdued colors are used in the background or recesses of a space. This creates a stage set effect where recesses appear deeper than they actually are.

Fig. 2.5

The pure blue of the soffit is the dominant color while the blue-gray of the tile is subordinate. The blue-gray tile appears to recede because it is the subordinate color. This gives dramatic emphasis to the apparent depth of the tile recess.

DOMINANT VALUES

Lighter values advance and dominate while darker values recede. This is because more light is reflected off lighter-value colors which makes them more luminous and draws the attention of the eye.

This principle can be applied to an interior to highlight the most important areas of the space. If an interior has medium to dark values and a few light accents the eye will naturally be drawn to these lighter areas. Hence, it is important to be selective about what to highlight with lighter value accents.

The lighter value of gold in the room beyond dominates while the darker gold value in the foreground recedes. This color effect focuses attention on the room beyond and makes it very inviting.

Fig. 2.6

The strongest color, red, is used in the smallest amount as an accent. The deep green, which is next strongest, is used in slightly greater amounts as an accent. The soft peach tone is used in the largest area.

HINT # 1

Use the strongest color in the smallest amount.

PROPORTIONS OF COLOR

As a general rule in designing colors for interiors, it is prudent to use the strongest or most dominant colors in the smallest amounts, otherwise, they tend to overpower the space and actually can become oppressive. When stronger colors are used in smaller amounts they function as accents and serve to enliven the more muted or neutral colors.

Fig. 2.7/2.8 *Recommended proportions of color based on their hierarchy of dominance are shown in the top figure. Note the dramatic difference in effect when the proportions of colors are reversed.*

This crisp, sunny interior offers an ideal example of effective color hierarchy. The lively yellow accent in this space is the strongest color but it is used in the smallest amounts. The rich, leaf green is the second strongest color and is used in slightly greater amounts. The least strong color is the soft, cream color of the walls. The mellow golden tones of the floor provide a harmonious base for all the other colors in the space.

The overall tonality of this bathroom is tan and white as these are the dominant colors, or the colors used in the greatest amounts. The smaller amounts of greens, blues, and rose tones provide rich accents. These are the subordinate colors.

TONALITY—WHICH COLOR DOMINATES?

As we have seen in the examples, the relative proportions of colors can affect which color dominates. Generally, the color that is used in the greatest proportion in any color scheme defines the *tonality* of the scheme. The color that defines the tonality of the scheme is the *dominant* color. The next most prominent color would be the *subdominant* color, and the color that is used the least, or used as an accent, is called the *subordinate* color.

As can be seen in the photo on the left, even a deep, warm color which would ordinarily dominate becomes subordinate when used in small amounts. So, as we have seen in the previous examples, the relative dominance of a color in a scheme is dependent on which colors are selected as well as on how much of each color is used.

Understanding the hierarchies of both the relative strength and the relative proportions of colors is important. This concept is essential to interior color design since an error in judgment becomes magnified when applied to a large area. Understanding and then effectively manipulating color hierarchies can produce outstanding results.

HINT # 2

The larger the area the stronger a color will appear.

Fig. 2.9

HOW INTENSE SHOULD A COLOR BE?

A small color swatch, no matter how accurate, always ends up being deceptive. It is difficult to visualize the effect of a color in a large area when you are selecting that color from a swatch measuring only a few square inches. The larger the area, the stronger a color will appear. What looked mostly gray with only a touch of lavender cast in a small chip can end up looking like a sickly purple when spread over an entire room. When in doubt, always opt for the more muted color, especially if there will be a lot of it.

To avoid this problem, always work from the largest color samples you can find. Whenever possible, test the color in a small area of the space. Always make sure that the sample color is viewed in the final location of the finished color. If it is a floor covering, then view the sample on the floor. A ceiling color sample should be viewed on the ceiling. The reason for this is that each different surface in the room receives a different amount and quality of light. As an experiment, hold a color sample on the ceiling and then place the same sample on the floor. For the most part, the sample on the ceiling will look considerably darker because there is less direct light. For this reason, it is better to err on the light side with color selections for the ceiling. It is also helpful to view the samples in both daylight and in whatever the source of artificial light will be.

COLOR PLACEMENT IN PERIOD INTERIORS

Knowing *where* to put color in a historical or period style interior is as important as understanding how to design color combinations. A well-coordinated collection of colors is only effective if the colors are placed in the interior so that the right architectural elements are emphasized or deemphasized. Even a very simple two-color scheme in a period interior can bring out the details of cornices, moldings, and columns.

Highlighting certain details can often help organize a room and give it scale. It can reduce the apparent ceiling height of a monumentally tall room or it can simplify and unify a room that suffers from an excess of complicated detail.

This period interior makes use of cool accents played off of the warm, creamy base colors of the walls and floors. The color values are reasonably close together with the exception of a few, deep color accent bands. Closely related color values keep this otherwise compact space feeling clean and open.

The general rules of thumb when applying color to architectural details in period interiors are as follows:

PROJECTIONS

In any color scheme, the dominant colors and lighter values or colors which advance should be on those details that project out into the space. This will make projecting molding profiles, column capitals, and raised panels seem to have even more pronounced three-dimensional qualities and will add drama and character to the space.

RECESSES

Subordinate colors and darker values—those which appear to recede—should be placed in recesses to emphasize the depth of the detail. This accentuates the natural shadow effect of the recesses. Avoid putting dominant colors in the recesses (and subordinate colors on the projections) as this tends to flatten out the architectural detail instead of emphasizing its three-dimensional depth.

Many of the architectural details in this ornate, period interior are highlighted with extremely subtle yet effective accent colors. All of the color values are similar so that the room retains a pleasant unity and simplicity. Note that there are continuous bands of color being highlighted, rather than individual carvings and details, which would make the interior very fussy and busy.

The details on this newel post are highlighted with beige in the recesses and off-white on the projections. This emphasizes the three-dimensional depth of the detailing. The value difference between the colors is just enough to be discernible.

33

High-style Victorian interiors were often a florid display of color and pattern. The papered walls and ceiling of this bedroom have a strong and cohesive, olive-and-burgundy tonality which unifies the room and its furnishings.

This period bathroom incorporates a broad array of color and decorative patterns in its free use of wallpaper and borders to create a whimsical fantasy. Sometimes it's worth ignoring all the decorating rules.

34

When in doubt, keep the overall color scheme simple and subdued. The goal is to highlight the architectural detail without overpowering it. Begin by accenting the details that are continuous around the room such as cornice moldings, picture rails, and chair rails. This keeps the accented lines continuous and simple. Avoid picking out each panel molding or door or window frame because this can break up the space and make it feel busy.

COLOR PLACEMENT IN CONTEMPORARY INTERIORS

The general rules of thumb when applying color to contemporary interiors follow.

THE DESIGN INTENT

Try to understand the design intent of the space before deciding where to place the colors. If there is some unifying design element in the space such as a soffit or other consistent design detail, it may be appropriate to subtly highlight it with color. Contemporary interiors are usually composed of abstract, intersecting lines, planes, and volumes which do not form neat, little box-like rooms or neatly framed and contained architectural detail. Play up the open-ended, interconnecting qualities of the space with the color placement.

The diagonal soffit above the entrance to the kitchen serves as a transition between the kitchen and the main space. The accent color on the soffit ties the colors together in the two areas.

The walls of this simple contemporary interior are treated as separate planes with individual accent colors.

This interior is composed of strong, graphic, abstract planes and volumes. The color placement in the interior carries this design approach through to its logical conclusion. The colors, like the geometry, are strong and graphic.

PLANES AND VOLUMES

If the interior is broken up into abstract planes and volumes, try treating each major plane or volume with a slightly different color. Effective color placement in such an interior can simplify and clarify the visual logic of the space. Without any color, this type of space can feel barren or chaotic. Often, it is most effective to use a low contrast color scheme in a space like this. Each color should be discernably different from its neighbor without resorting to jarring contrasts.

ACCENT ELEMENTS

Accent colors may be used to draw attention to any special architectural features, such as railings, cabinetry, or millwork. It may be appropriate to employ stronger contrasts when selecting these accents; be sure that the particular architectural element selected is the proper one to highlight.

Each architectural element in the space at the right functions as an accent and each has its own distinct yet harmonious color. The bright yellow in the recesses of the cabinet give the room an unexpected vibrancy. Although there are many similarities between the colors in this interior and the colors in the photo below, the effect is quite different. The deep blue here forms a rich backdrop against which everything else is displayed, as though one is looking at jewelry inside a blue velvet case.

COLOR HARMONY

The most fundamental theory of color harmony in interior design is to make sure that the colors in any color scheme share some common traits or attributes. Remember that colors have three attributes:

1. Hue or Color
2. Value or Lightness
3. Chroma or Saturation

Maintaining some similarities between colors ensures that they relate to each other and are thereby harmonious. Once a harmonious base color combination is established, add dramatic accents to enliven the color scheme and prevent it from being boring.

HINT # 3

Only vary one color attribute at a time.

SIMILAR HUE AND VALUE

An easy way to achieve color harmony is to keep the **hue** and **value** the same while varying the **chroma**. This means that the color scheme employs variations of a single color of a single relative lightness or darkness and that the intensity of the color is varied. Some of the colors might be more full bodied while others are more grayed down.

or

SIMILAR HUE AND CHROMA

Another way to achieve color harmony is to keep the **hue** and **chroma** the same and vary the **value**. This type of scheme would include variations of the same color at the same intensity with only the relative lightness or darkness of the color changing.

or

Similar hue and chroma. *This is a very safe and simple approach to color. The colors are all in the peach-beige family with only the relative color values varied. The strongest values are in the smallest amounts, creating an overall effect that is soft and harmonious.*

SIMILAR VALUE AND CHROMA

Yet another way to achieve color harmony is to keep the **value** and **chroma** the same and vary the **hue.** In this case the relative lightness or darkness would remain the same, as well as the saturation level of the color, and only the hue or actual color would vary. Surprisingly, this last technique often is underutilized. By keeping the value and chroma constant and the colors slightly grayed (medium chroma), one can put together virtually any combination of colors to create extraordinarily complex schemes which are at the same time remarkably calm and harmonious.

Similar hue and value. Note that the furniture in this light and airy interior is a grayed-down version of the wall and ceiling color. The hue and value remain constant and only the chroma varies.

Similar value and chroma. This bedroom includes an unlikely combination of colors yet they harmonize quite well. One main key to success here is that each color is precisely the same value and chroma. Only the hues themselves are varied.

MONOTONE SCHEMES

A monotone color scheme consists of various tints or shades of a single neutral color such as gray, beige, or cream. This type of color scheme is a safe and conservative approach to interior color design. It is also very effective when a variety of natural materials and textures are incorporated into the interior, as this allows these materials to take center stage.

NEUTRAL MONOTONE SCHEMES

A neutral, monotone color scheme is by far the most foolproof and conservative approach to decorating an interior. It allows the objects and artwork in the space to take the forefront by providing a simple, unobtrusive backdrop. A truly neutral, monotone color scheme is neither warm nor cool; rather, it is entirely neutral as the description implies. It would include shades of white, off-white, and neutral grays and create a very serious and sophisticated ambiance in the space. Feelings evoked by this color design might include calm, businesslike, aloof, subtle, subdued, clean, austere, stark.

COOL MONOTONE SCHEMES

Cool monotone schemes might include green-grays, blue-grays, lavender-grays, or cool off-whites. A cool monotone interior tends to feel more airy, atmospheric, and light than a warm monotone interior. To avoid unpleasant starkness, furnishings can provide a few warm accents for balance.

Neutral monotone schemes. *The photograph on the facing page shows a particularly effective use of neutral grays to create an austere yet pleasing space.*

Cool monotone schemes. *The ice blue, monotone color scheme has a refreshing, atmospheric quality. The warm orange and yellow accents intensify the cool depths of blue.*

Warm monotone schemes. *The muted bronze colors in the classic monotone interior at the left are further enriched by the natural wood tones of the furniture.*

Frank Lloyd Wright's original home and studio incorporates muted, neutral earth tones which harmonize with the wood tones.

42

This elegantly abstract space blurs the distinction between inside and outside. The colors both define individual architectural elements in the space and weave the space together.

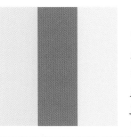

The bright, contrasting colors create a lively layered effect in this contemporary interior. The progression from yellow-green to yellow to red-orange heightens the sense layering.

COMPLEMENTARY SCHEMES

Complementary colors, or contrasting hues, are those found directly opposite each other on the color wheel. Complementary color schemes are often the most striking and lively yet the most difficult to execute well because a misjudgment in color selection can cause the scheme to be jarring. Study successful examples of complementary color schemes to understand what works and what doesn't. Designs using complementary colors are often described as exciting, cheerful, energetic, and vibrant.

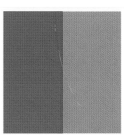

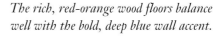

The rich, red-orange wood floors balance well with the bold, deep blue wall accent.

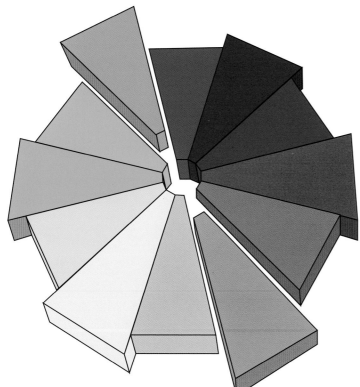

Fig. 3.3 *Complementary colors*

The cool, blue-green accent balances the smooth, warm ocher color of this kitchen and prevents the ocher from overpowering the room.

The weathered, blue-green walls are a strong but balanced contrast to the pale peach above.

SPLIT COMPLEMENTARY

A split complement is one hue on one side of the color wheel and the two hues on either side of its complement. Split complements are always vibrant, almost too vibrant, but they can also be very effective.

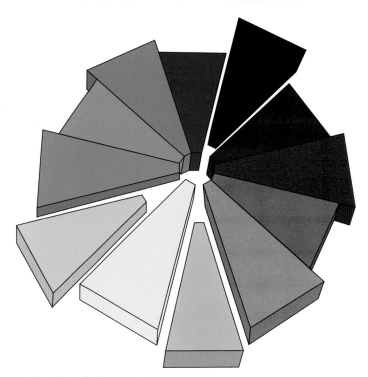

Fig. 3.4 *Split complements*

The yellow-green of the walls and the yellow-orange of ceiling and woodwork, in combination with the deep purple of the carpet, provide an excellent example of a successful split complement color scheme.

50

The multitude of colors and textures in yellow-orange, red, and blue in this interior create a complex yet unified color environment. The natural wood tones are skillfully woven into the entire color scheme.

This powerful color scheme uses full intensity colors for startling drama.

TRIADS

A triad consists of any three equidistant colors on the color wheel. The primary colors red, yellow, and blue form the most common triad. Primary colors can be very stimulating in a child's environment as children respond to strong colors in their early stages of development. For an adult to live with nothing but primary colors for a long time could become tedious. When muted or lightened, triads can create very rich, satisfying schemes which are more appealing to an adult's color sophistication.

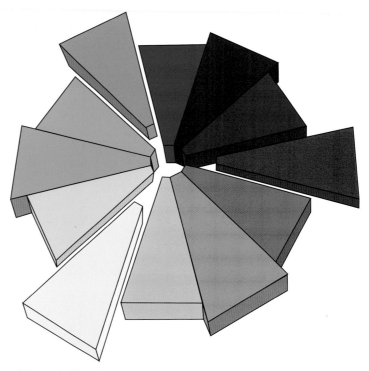

Fig. 3.5 *Triads*

This kitchen is done in primary colors but has a radically different feel than the photo on the bottom of page 51.. Here, the colors are soft and grayed down to create a very subtle but richly balanced scheme. The deep reds prevent the other colors from appearing too washed out.

The full intensity of these primary colors brings to mind a tropical environment.

The simple, abstract geometry of this space combined with strong primary colors has a riveting graphic quality. The red at the end of the corridor draws the eye, even though there is only a small amount of the color showing.

TETRADS

A tetrad is any two pairs of complements. Tetrads are by far the most challenging to master in color design. Tetrads are often used in fabric, wallpaper, or other decorative designs where the colors can be interlaced together for balance and harmony.

The kitchen has a neutral background of white against which red wood tones and green paint provide complementary contrast. The blue door and orange wood tones are also complementary hues.

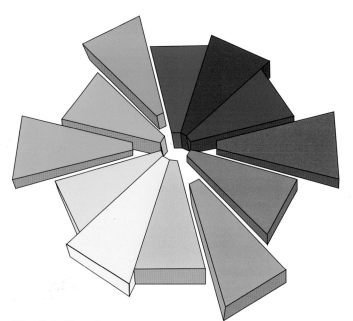

Fig. 3.6 *Tetrads*

This unusual color scheme combines red and green complements with blue and wood tone orange complements. The color of the furnishings is simple so that it does not compete with the other colors.

55

DISCORDANT COLORS FOR SPECIAL EFFECT

Sometimes bending or breaking the rules of color harmony is useful and very effective. So far, all of the color harmony principles discussed describe fairly symmetrical color balance. If these principles are followed rigorously, harmonious combinations will be achieved. However, perfect color harmony can be boring and predictable. Sometimes bending or breaking the rules of color harmony is useful and very effective. A strong discordant color thrown into a scheme can make the design more dynamic.

Discordant colors can also be used to boldly grab attention or to add an element of surprise. The important consideration is whether the color is drawing attention to the right thing at the right time. As a color designer gains knowledge and experience, the designs may become more adventurous.

This kitchen on the facing page is composed of many warm earthtones. The blue accent walls provide a welcome relief to all the warm colors.

The seat covers in this dining room provide multicolor accents which are a delightful surprise in an otherwise subdued room.

This most unusual interior incorporates
virtually every color in the color wheel.
The room looks like ribbon candy,
an edible fantasy.

This lively triad color scheme consists
of yellow-orange, blue-green, and purple-
red. The addition of vibrant, discordant
accents make this space feel very active.

These discordant colors are reminiscent of high-style interiors from the 1960s. The effect is wonderfully stylized and theatrical.

PART II

THE COLOR SAMPLES

The following examples are intended to spark the imagination and provide a starting point for the color designer. It would be impossible to show an example of every possible color scheme. The possible color combinations and effects are limited only by the skill and imagination of the designer. This chapter, however, covers all of the basic color scheme categories. For each section, a sample color combination is shown in a sample interior which illustrates the flavor and character of the type of color combination being shown. Additional color combinations are then displayed in chip form. These other schemes could just as easily be substituted into the photo shown. This visualization tool should enable the designer and homeowner to imagine and design many variations on a theme, either by copying the actual color chip combinations or by inventing new variations. The color samples form a library of potential color schemes for ready reference.

 MONOTONE
NEUTRAL MONOTONES

MONOTONE
WARM MONOTONE

 MONOTONE
COOL MONOTONE

 MONOCHROMATIC
RED

 MONOCHROMATIC
RED-ORANGE

 MONOCHROMATIC
ORANGE

MONOCHROMATIC
YELLOW–ORANGE

 MONOCHROMATIC
YELLOW

 MONOCHROMATIC
YELLOW-GREEN

78

 MONOCHROMATIC
GREEN

 MONOCHROMATIC
BLUE-GREEN

 MONOCHROMATIC
PURPLE

 ANALOGOUS
RED, RED-ORANGE, ORANGE

 ANALOGOUS
ORANGE, YELLOW-ORANGE, YELLOW

 ANALOGOUS
YELLOW-ORANGE, YELLOW, YELLOW-GREEN

 ANALOGOUS
YELLOW-ORANGE, YELLOW, YELLOW-GREEN

 ANALOGOUS
GREEN, BLUE-GREEN, BLUE

 ANALOGOUS
BLUE-GREEN, BLUE, BLUE-PURPLE

 ANALOGOUS
PURPLE, RED-PURPLE, RED

 COMPLEMENTARY
RED AND GREEN

 COMPLEMENTARY
YELLOW AND PURPLE

 COMPLEMENTARY
ORANGE AND BLUE

118

 COMPLEMENTARY
ORANGE AND BLUE

120

 SPLIT COMPLEMENTARY
RED-ORANGE, GREEN, BLUE

 SPLIT COMPLEMENTARY
YELLOW-ORANGE, RED-ORANGE, BLUE

 SPLIT COMPLEMENTARY
YELLOW-ORANGE, RED-ORANGE, BLUE

 SPLIT COMPLEMENTARY
ORANGE, BLUE-GREEN, BLUE-PURPLE

130

 **TRIADS**
YELLOW, BLUE, RED

 TRIADS
YELLOW, BLUE, RED

 TRIADS
YELLOW-ORANGE, BLUE-GREEN,
PURPLE-RED

 **TETRADS**
RED, ORANGE, BLUE, GREEN

138

 TETRADS
RED, ORANGE, BLUE, GREEN

140

TETRADS
RED, ORANGE, BLUE, GREEN

142

DISCORDANT

144

DISCORDANT

146

GLOSSARY

ADDITIVE COLOR

Process of mixing colored light. The primary colors of red, green, and blue light make white light when mixed together.

ANALOGOUS COLORS

Analogous colors are adjacent to each other on the color wheel.

CHROMA

Also referred to as saturation. Chroma is the relative strength or weakness of a color.

COMPLEMENTARY COLORS

Colors which are opposite each other on the color wheel, such as red and green.

COOL COLORS

Blue-green, blue, and blue-purple are cool colors.

HUE

Hue is the name of a color.

MONOCHROMATIC

A monochromatic color scheme employs various tints and shades of a single color.

MONOTONE

A monotone or neutral color scheme consists of various tints and shades of a neutral color.

NEUTRAL COLOR

A color that appears neither warm nor cool, such as gray.

PARTITIVE COLOR

Color which is created by mixing many small dots of color which then appear to the eye as a single new color.

PRIMARY COLORS

The primary colors of pigments and dyes are red, yellow, and blue. All other colors are derived from these three.

SATURATION

Also referred to as chroma, see CHROMA.

SHADE

A color created by adding black to a hue.

SPLIT COMPLEMENTARY COLORS

Split complementary colors are made up of any color combined with the two colors on either side of its complement.

SUBTRACTIVE COLOR

The process of mixing pigments, inks, or dyes. The primary subtractive colors are red, yellow, and blue from which all other colors are derived.

TETRAD

A tetrad is any two pairs of complementary colors.

TINT

A color created by adding white to a hue.

TONE

A color created by adding gray to a hue.

TONALITY

The overall impression made by the dominant color in a color scheme.

TRIAD

A triad of colors is any three equidistant colors on the color wheel. The primary colors, red, yellow, and blue form a triad.

VALUE

The relative lightness or darkness of a color.

WARM COLOR

Red, orange, and yellow are warm colors.

151

BIBLIOGRAPHY

Amos, Gwen. "Color Theory in Practice." *Step By Step Graphics* 7, No. 2 (March/April 1991): 74–83.

Eckstein, Helene. "Understanding Basic Color Concepts." *Step By Step Graphics* 7, No. 2 (March/April 1991): 62–69.

Eiseman, Leatrice, and Lawrence Herbert. *The PANTONE Book of Color.* New York: Harry N. Abrams, Inc., 1990.

Faulkner, Waldron. *Architecture and Color.* New York: Wiley-Interscience, 1972.

Fishel, Catharine. "The Psychology of Color." *Step By Step Graphics* 7, No. 2 (March/April 1991): 84–91.

Gerstner, Karl. *The Forms of Color: The Interaction of Visual Elements.* Cambridge: The MIT Press, 1986.

Itten, Johannes. *The Color Star.* New York: Van Nostrand Reinhold, 1985.

Lena, Nicholas M. "Light and Color Evaluation." *Step By Step Graphics* 7, No. 2 (March/April 1991): 70–73.

Munsell, A. H. *A Color Notation.* Baltimore: Macbeth, A Division of Kollmorgen Corporation, 1981.

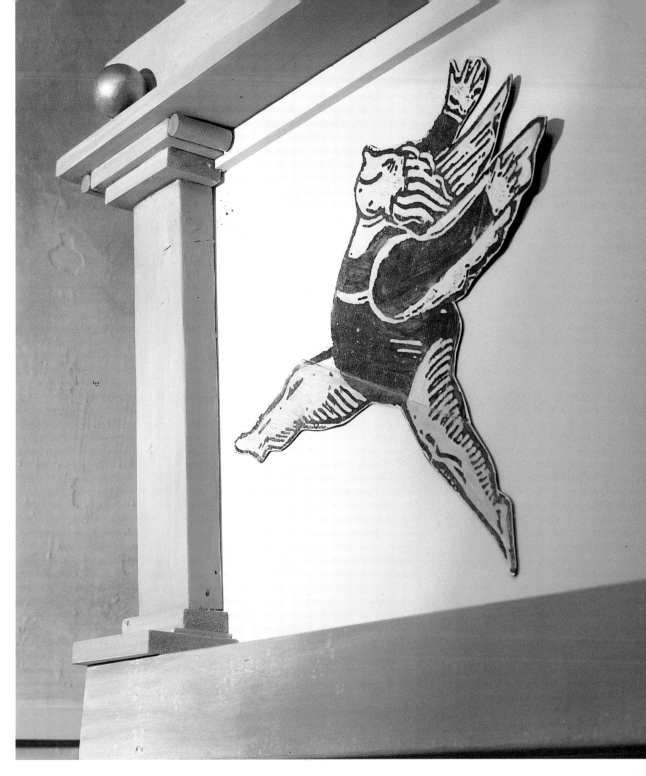

ABOUT THE AUTHOR

Jonathan Poore is an architectural designer, illustrator, and writer. His work has appeared in *The Journal of Light Construction*, *The Naturally Elegant Home* by Janet Marinelli (Little, Brown), *The New York Times*, *Old-House Journal*, *Progressive Architecture*, and other publications. He provides color consulting in both residential and commercial settings, and enjoys weaving color integrally into all aspects of design.

159

ACKNOWLEDGMENTS

I wish to thank Brenda Edgar and Carolyn Benson for their help with the monumental task of photo research and cataloging. Special thanks to Jason Gove for his patience in unraveling the mysteries of our new computer programs which were used to draw the illustrations. Credit goes to Steve Bridges, Rosalie Grattaroti, and Julie Cleveland at Rockport Publishers for assisting with the development and editing of the book. Thanks also goes to Sara Day, the book designer, who was a key player in pulling the project together into a cohesive whole. Finally, I wish to dedicate this book to Sharon and Samantha Adams in gratitude for their support and patience.